LEVEL 1

MARVEL

STORM
DISASTER ALERT!

Daka Hermon

NATIONAL GEOGRAPHIC

Washington, D.C.

Illustrated by Ron Lim
with colors by Israel Silva

To my dad, Joseph, who taught me how to weather many storms —Daka

Published by National Geographic Partners, LLC, Washington, DC 20036.

Designed by Gustavo Tello

Trade paperback ISBN: 978-1-4263-7824-9
Reinforced library binding ISBN:
978-1-4263-7825-6

The author and publisher gratefully acknowledge the literacy review of this book by Mariam Jean Dreher, professor emerita of reading education, University of Maryland, College Park, and expert review by Dr. George Kourounis.

Art Credits
Illustrated by Ron Lim with colors by Israel Silva

Photo Credits
ALL MARVEL CHARACTERS, ARTWORK, AND LOGOS © 2025 MARVEL

Cover: (LE), stnazkul/Adobe Stock; 1 (BACKGROUND), Wira SHK/Shutterstock; 1 (LO), Lynsey Addario/National Geographic Image Collection; 1 (UP LE), Alexander Gogolin/Adobe Stock; 1 (UP RT), Minerva Studio/Shutterstock; 3 (UP LE), Alex/Adobe Stock; 3 (UP RT), selim/Adobe Stock; 7 (LO), John Sirlin/Alamy Stock Photo; 8, Christian/Adobe Stock; 10, Francisco/Adobe Stock; 10-11, Tom Wang/Adobe Stock; 11 (UP), vanildo/Adobe Stock; 11 (LO), F Armstrong Photo/Adobe Stock; 12, Lynsey Addario/National Geographic Image Collection; 13, fauzan/Adobe Stock; 14-15, JSirlin/Adobe Stock; 16, zenobillis/Adobe Stock; 17, Satoshi Kina/Adobe Stock; 18 (UP LE), 24K-Production/Adobe Stock; 18 (UP RT), MarkusBar/Shutterstock; 18 (LO), Léopold/Adobe Stock; 18-19, valdezrl/Adobe Stock; 19 (UP), Detlev Van Ravensway/Science Source; 19 (CTR), Minerva Studio/Shutterstock; 19 (LO), OSORIOartist/Adobe Stock; 20, Thomas Dutour/Adobe Stock; 21, burakguralp/Shutterstock; 22, Stocktrek Images/National Geographic Image Collection; 23, Islamic Footage/Shutterstock; 24-25, Sadatsugo Tomizawa/AFP/Getty Images; 26 (LO), DenisTangneyJr/Getty Images; 27, eddtoro/Shutterstock; 28, Kirill/Adobe Stock; 30 (LE), valdezrl/Adobe Stock; 30 (RT), Maygutyak/Adobe Stock; 31 (UP LE), Michel/Adobe Stock; 31 (UP RT), Uheheu/Shutterstock; 31 (LO LE), Blue/Adobe Stock; 31 (LO RT), Achira22/Adobe Stock; 32 (UP LE), Fotos 593/Adobe Stock; 32 (UP RT), mbruxelle/Adobe Stock; 32 (LO LE), whitcomberd/Adobe Stock; 32 (LO RT), IgorZh/Adobe Stock

Printed in the United States of America
25/WOR/1

Contents

Super Storm

Which super hero can control the weather? Storm, that's who!

Storm and her friends have the same super-powers as natural disasters. Follow along to learn what happens when disaster strikes!

Thunderstorm

Storm's friend Thor knows that a thunderstorm has lightning and thunder. Kaboom! Thunder is the sound that lightning makes when it heats up the air.

STORM TIP: When the weather roars, go indoors. If it is thunder you hear, lightning is near.

Lightning is a gigantic spark of electricity in the clouds. Lightning bolts are super hot. The villain Electro uses his power to light up the sky!

I'M ELECTRIFYING!

Flood

Watch out! The villain Hydro-Man has turned himself into a flood.

A flood happens when a lot of water rushes over dry land.

Heavy rainfall from thunderstorms can cause flooding.

Flash floods are floods that happen fast. They can damage bridges, roads, cars, and buildings.

THE WEATHER FORECAST CALLS FOR LOTS OF RAIN.

Drought

What happens when the weather heats up like Human Torch and there's not enough rain or snow? A drought (DROUT).

A drought can last months or years. A heat wave can make a drought worse.

Storm can help! She has the power to make it rain.

SEVERE DROUGHT
CONSERVE WATER

STORM TIP:
Help save water! Take short showers instead of baths, or wash dishes in the dishwasher instead of by hand.

STORMY Words

HEAT WAVE: Very hot weather that lasts for more than two days

Wildfire

Fires can start when heat, oxygen, and fuel come together. Hot and dry weather sometimes causes wildfires in forests or grasslands.

Wildfires move fast like Firestar. These fires are very hot and dangerous. Most wildfires start when humans are not careful with fire or when lightning strikes.

Tornado

Is that Mr. Fantastic racing across the plains? No, it's a tornado!

A tornado is a cone of twisting air that stretches from the sky to the ground. It is also called a twister.

Twisters happen when warm, wet air and cold, dry air come together.

I KNOW HOW TO TWIST AND STRETCH, TOO!

STORM TIP:
If there's a tornado, take cover in the lowest part of your house and put your hands over your head and neck. Stay away from windows and doors.

Hurricane

Look out, Namor! A hurricane is headed your way. Hurricanes are storms that form over warm water in tropical parts of the ocean. They have strong winds and heavy rains.

HURRICANES CAN BE REALLY DESTRUCTIVE!

The center of a hurricane is called the eye. The most powerful part of the hurricane is just outside the eye.

17

6 DISASTER FACTS

1
WILDFIRES MOVE FASTER UPHILL THAN DOWNHILL.

2
THE FEAR OF LIGHTNING AND THUNDER IS CALLED ASTRAPHOBIA (AS-TRUH-FOH-BEE-UH).

I AM QUITE FOND OF BLUE.

3
LIGHTNING COMES IN MANY COLORS. BLUE IS ONE OF THE HOTTEST COLORS!

MARS HAS THE LARGEST VOLCANO IN OUR SOLAR SYSTEM. IT'S CALLED OLYMPUS MONS, AND IT ERUPTED A VERY LONG TIME AGO.

I ONCE LIVED ON MARS!

4

5

MOST OF THE WORLD'S TORNADOES OCCUR IN AN AREA OF THE UNITED STATES THAT'S NICKNAMED TORNADO ALLEY. UP TO 1,200 TORNADOES CAN FORM THERE EACH YEAR.

6

HURRICANES ARE NAMED IN ALPHABETICAL ORDER, BUT THEY NEVER START WITH Q, U, X, Y, OR Z.

Earthquake

LET'S ROCK AND ROLL!

Super hero Quake likes to get things shaking! But earthquakes come from inside Earth.

Tectonic plates are like giant puzzle pieces that make up Earth's surface. Sometimes tectonic plates get stuck and then move suddenly. That causes earthquakes.

STORM TIP: During an earthquake, drop, cover, and hold on!

Volcano

Volcanoes are openings in Earth's surface. When there is a lot of pressure inside a volcano, it erupts!

STORMY Words

ERUPT: To release ash, gas, and lava

Ash and steam fill the air. Really hot liquid rock called lava flows out of the volcano. Like Molten Man, lava is so hot it can burn anything in its path.

ARGH! TIME TO BLOW OFF SOME STEAM!

Tsunami

Earthquakes and underwater volcanic eruptions can make giant waves. These waves are called tsunamis (soo-NAH-meez).

Tsunami waves can be more than 100 feet (30.5 m) tall. A tsunami can move as fast as an airplane— 600 miles an hour (966 km/h)!

Winter Weather

What is Iceman's favorite type of weather? Ice storms!

Ice storms happen when super-cold rain freezes.

Storm's frosty foe Blizzard is blowing in. Blizzards are big snowstorms with chilly winds.

It is very important to stay inside where it is warm during a blizzard.

STORM TIP: Have a flashlight ready! Winter storms can damage power lines and shut off power.

Avalanche

I CAN UPROOT TREES AND DESTROY ANIMAL HABITATS!

What is Avalanche's favorite natural disaster? An avalanche! An avalanche is a huge amount of snow and ice that slides quickly down a mountain.

Earthquakes, snowstorms, animals, snowboarders, skiers, and other things that move can start an avalanche.

STORM AND HER FRIENDS KNOW HOW STRONG
NATURAL DISASTERS CAN BE. NOW YOU DO, TOO.
SHARE WITH YOUR FRIENDS WHAT YOU'VE LEARNED
ABOUT HOW POWERFUL NATURE CAN BE!

What in the World?

These pictures are close-up views of natural disasters. Use the hints to help figure out what's in the pictures. Answers are on page 31.

1 HINT: This can cause wildfires.

2 **HINT:** This is when snow slides down a mountain.

Word Bank

tsunami wave   eye   drought   avalanche

lava   lightning

3

HINT: This can be more than 100 feet (30.5 m) tall.

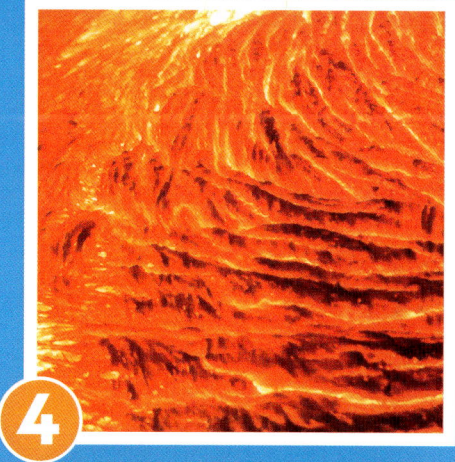

4

HINT: This flows from volcanoes.

5

HINT: This is the center of a hurricane.

6

HINT: This happens when there is not enough rain.

GLOSSARY

ERUPT: TO RELEASE ASH, GAS, AND LAVA

HEAT WAVE: VERY HOT WEATHER THAT LASTS FOR MORE THAN TWO DAYS

NATURAL DISASTER: A DANGEROUS EVENT IN NATURE

WEATHER: WHAT IT IS LIKE OUTSIDE AT ONE PLACE AND TIME